S0-AAD-997

598.72
MAR

Mara, Wil
Woodpeckers

FE 19 '95			
29 - AP			
DE 7 '96			
DE 0	FEB 0 6 20		
DE 2 9 '96	MAR 1 7		
FEB 1 3 20			

ANNIE E VINTON ELEMENTARY
SCHOOL LIBRARY
306 STAFFORD ROAD
MANSFIELD CENTER, CT 06250

Woodpeckers

Wil Mara

Cavendish Square

New York

Published in 2015 by Cavendish Square Publishing, LLC
243 5th Avenue, Suite 136, New York, NY 10016

Website: cavendishsq.com

This publication represents the opinions and views of the author based on his or her personal experience, knowledge, and research. The information in this book serves as a general guide only. The author and publisher have used their best efforts in preparing this book and disclaim liability rising directly or indirectly from the use and application of this book.

CPSIA Compliance Information: Batch #WS14CSQ

All websites were available and accurate when this book was sent to press.

Library of Congress Cataloging-in-Publication Data

Mara, Wil, author.
Woodpeckers / Wil Mara.
pages cm. — (Backyard safari)
Includes index.
ISBN 978-1-62712-837-7 (hardcover) ISBN 978-1-62712-838-4 (paperback) ISBN 978-1-62712-839-1 (ebook)
1. Woodpeckers—Juvenile literature. I. Title.
QL696.P56M35 2015
598.7'2—dc23
2013050616

Editorial Director: Dean Miller
Editor: Andrew Coddington
Copy Editor: Cynthia Roby
Art Director: Jeffrey Talbot
Designer: Joseph Macri
Photo Researcher: J8 Media
Production Manager: Jennifer Ryder-Talbot
Production Editor: David McNamara

The photographs in this book are used by permission and through the courtesy of: Cover photo by liewwk - www.liewwkphoto.com/Flickr/Getty Images; panda3800/Shutterstock.com, 4; Menno Schaefer/Shutterstock.com, 5; Wendy Sue Gilman/Shutterstock.com, 6; © Papilio/Alamy 7; John Cancalosi/Photolibrary/Getty Images, 8; George Grall/National Geographic/Getty Images, 10; kali9/E+/Getty Images, 11; Grant Glendinning/Shutterstock.com, 14; BrianLasenby/iStock/Thinkstock, 16; MidwestWilderness/E+/Getty Images, 19; StevenRussellSmithPhotos/Shutterstock.com, 21; Picoides pubescens by Male Pileated Woodpecker feeding on tree by Joshlaymon under CC BY 2.0, 21; Wolfgang Wander is licensed under CC BY 2.0, 21; ElementalImaging/E+/Getty Images, 21; Dennis Lane/Photolibrary/Getty Images, 22; Jan Vermeer/Foto Natura/Minden Pictures/Getty Images, 23; Oleksandr Berezko/Shutterstock.com, 25; ©iStockphoto.com/busypix, 27.

Printed in the United States of America

Contents

Introduction

Have you ever watched a squirrel chasing another squirrel around a tree, or a group of deer leaping gracefully through a stretch of winter woods? If you have, then you know how wonderful it is to discover nature for yourself. Each book in the Backyard Safari series takes you step-by-step on an easy outdoor adventure, and then helps you identify the animals you've found. You'll also learn ways to attract, observe, and protect these valuable creatures. As you read, be on the lookout for the Safari Tips and Trek Talk facts sprinkled throughout the book. Ready? The fun starts just steps from your back door!

ONE

A Woodpecker's Life

The woodpecker is named for the way it uses its bill to "peck" into trees to find insects. It also drums into tree trunks to create a nesting area, as a sign of marking its territory, and to store food. The North American species of woodpecker is considered medium-sized. Its average length measures from 10 to 20 inches (25 to 51 centimeters) and its **wingspan**, about 12 to 21 inches (30 to 53 cm). The

A woodpecker may peck on a wood surface, such as trees, for a variety of reasons.

adult bird weighs approximately 10 to 15 ounces (28 to 43 kilograms). Coloration of the woodpecker's plumage can be white, black, brown, or green. More brilliant colors cover its head, red being among the most common. These bright colors are used for everything from frightening off **predators** to signaling other woodpeckers.

The woodpecker's most outstanding physical feature is its long, pointed bill, which remains tough and sharp in spite of its continual use. In fact, Pileated woodpeckers hammer into trees with a speed of 15 miles (24 kilometers) per hour—20 times per second. Yet in spite of its constant pecking, a woodpecker never gets a headache. This is because its head is structured to protect the bird as it goes about its daily life. It has thick muscles, spongy bones, and a third eyelid that blocks dust and splinters. These keep its small brain intact. Also, woodpeckers don't peck for long periods at a time—only for a few seconds before taking a rest.

A woodpecker's head is designed to withstand the repeated impact of all the pecking it does.

The woodpecker wraps the tip of its tongue around small food items and pulls them from the hole it made. Depending on the species, the tongue may be barbed, or have a sharp point, which is helpful for removing insects. Most woodpeckers have **zygodactyl** feet, meaning that, of their four toes, two point forward and two face backward. The strength of the toes allows the bird to clamp onto trees and remain steady as it pecks. Its tail feathers are stiff, which also gives the woodpecker strong balance.

Where They Live

Woodpeckers are found everywhere except Australia and its surrounding areas, and the frigid polar regions. They are also absent from many islands in the ocean that are far from any continent. Because woodpeckers are so widespread and have a large number of **species**, they have adapted to live in diverse habitats. Although the birds prefer wooded places in the wild, they will occasionally venture into suburbs and rarely into cities. Woodpeckers have been found in **habitats** such as scrublands—land covered with small bushes and trees—tropical rain forests, deserts, grasslands, and savannas. Woodpeckers are usually **arboreal**, meaning

A woodpecker's toes are designed to give them a good grip.

they spend most of their time in trees. There are a few species that will fly down to forage for food, and a small number that nest in holes in the ground. But most woodpecker species remain in trees.

What They Do

Woodpeckers are **diurnal**, meaning they are active during the day and rest at night. They will often roost in tree holes they have created and may use different holes at different times. Depending on the species, woodpeckers may live solitary lives. These particular birds will not gather in flocks and can be nasty to other birds, including other woodpeckers. Other, more social species, however, do assemble in flocks. Some have even been known to mix with other bird species in large groups. This lifestyle provides them greater feeding opportunities and additional protection from predators.

Many woodpeckers are solitary, meaning they live alone.

Trek Talk

Woodpeckers are, as their name suggests, attracted to wood, particularly wood that **invertebrates** call home. Although woodpeckers spend most of their time in trees, they have also been known to peck at the outside wood structures of houses. If the structure of a home, for example, becomes infested with termites or ants, a woodpecker may swoop down and begin pecking in search of its next meal. While this may help control a bug problem, it will also cause the home considerable damage. Nevertheless, you might want to keep your eyes and ears open when you walk through your neighborhood.

Woodpeckers are **omnivorous**, which means they eat both plant and animal matter. Their favored **prey** is insects and insect larvae, which they find in trees that are both alive and dead. Woodpeckers are considered helpful to living trees because they feed on pests such as termites that cause the trees harm. They also feed on the sap, nuts, and fruits of living trees, and will forage the ground for food if nothing else is available.

The Cycle of Life

Woodpeckers breed during the spring in most parts of their **range**. They will nest within tree cavities that are generally oblong in shape, measuring from 10 to 24 inches (25.4 to 61 cm), and bored by the male. Construction of the nesting hole usually takes three to four weeks to complete. Because some other bird species also nest in tree holes, male woodpeckers often have to defend their territory. There are a few woodpecker species—specifically those that dwell in desert areas—that create their nesting holes in cacti. A tiny number even make nesting holes in the ground.

Both male and female woodpeckers care for young.

A woodpecker often remains with its mate for years at a time. After the female lays her eggs, both the male and female woodpeckers will care for them. The **clutch**, or nest of eggs, will number anywhere from two to six. Each egg, spherical in shape, is white with a glossy surface like porcelain. The eggs hatch within two weeks, at which time both parents will help feed and protect their young. It will take from two weeks to a full month for the chicks to leave the nest. The average lifespan of a woodpecker in the wild is about five to ten years, depending on the species.

TWO

You Are the Explorer

Millions of people around the world enjoy **ornithology**—the study of birds. Bird watching is a relaxing and rewarding outdoor activity. Woodpeckers make particularly interesting study subjects because of their beauty and interesting habits. They also seem fairly comfortable with humans nearby. Once you understand the importance of giving them their space and not disturbing them, you will begin to see for yourself the fascinating lives they lead.

What Do I Wear?

* Clothes that are not too bright or vivid in color. You don't want to disturb, distract, or frighten the woodpeckers.
* Old clothes that can get dirty, since you'll be outside.
* Clothes that are loose-fitting and comfortable.
* A jacket, gloves, hat, and other warm clothing, particularly if you are going on your safari during cold weather.
* Any type of shoes will do, but those with soft soles will be the quietest. Also, if you have to do a lot of walking, you'll want the shoes to be comfortable. In the winter, you may need boots.
* Bug spray, particularly if the climate is warmer and you're going into forested areas near waterways or in other sections known to have flying pests.

What Do I Take?

* Binoculars. You should never try to get too close to a live woodpecker. For the best view of the birds, a good pair of binoculars will be the most important piece of equipment you can bring along on your safari.
* Digital camera, particularly one that has strong zoom capability.
* Notebook
* Pen or pencil
* Folding chair or blanket
* A snack for yourself

Where Do I Go?

Woodpeckers can be found in a broad range of habitats. Most North American species, however, will need to be in wooded areas as they nest, roost, and forage for food in trees. They spend the majority of their time in the air, only coming down occasionally to search for food if nothing else is available. So remember, most of the woodpeckers you spot will either be flying around or clutched to the side of a large tree.

* The woods. Woodpeckers live in trees, so wooded areas are great places for your safari. Woodpeckers seem fairly comfortable around humans, but they don't prefer to be around them. If there is a large stretch of quiet, undeveloped woodland within a reasonable distance of your home, you'll have a better chance of finding woodpeckers there than anywhere else.

* Suburbs with some forestation. Woodpeckers generally avoid cities, but they will live in suburban areas as long as there are enough trees around. Even private homes with small forest patches on their property are suitable. As long as woodpeckers feel somewhat safe from potential predators and can keep

Woodpeckers spend most of their time off the ground and are often seen on tree branches.

Safari Tip

Woodpeckers are known to make sounds other than rapid-fire tapping and pecking. Because woodpeckers are **territorial**, they can also go into full-scale alarmed-and-annoyed mode, which can be quite noisy. If an unwelcome species of bird strays into their territory, woodpeckers will put up quite a fuss by squawking, flapping their wings, and jousting with their bill. Chances are the intruder will make quite a few noises, too! If you live in an area where you know there are woodpeckers as well as other bird species (which is likely), keep this in mind during your safari. Also keep in mind that woodpeckers can be short-tempered in the spring and early summer. During this time they have nests and young to protect.

a certain distance from human activity, they will settle down and go about their business.

❋ Desert areas with cacti. Some woodpeckers have adapted to life in the desert. These birds will make their homes and nest in cacti found there. If you happen to live in one of the North American desert areas, you can still go on a woodpecker safari! In fact, it's probably easier to locate a woodpecker in a cactus-spotted desert than in a forested area. There is less leaf cover, so you will be able to see more woodpeckers at a greater distance. Binoculars are very helpful in this environment.

You should never go on a woodpecker safari alone, so always make sure you are with a trusted adult. Also, if you plan to go on someone else's property, always get permission beforehand. Trespassing can get you into very serious trouble. Privately owned and natural forested regions, for example, are a great place to find woodpeckers—but not if you aren't allowed to be there.

What Do I Do?

❋ Go out during the day. Since woodpeckers are diurnal creatures, you won't find them during the night. You will need to start your safari very early in the morning if you want to see them when they're fully rested and ready for their daily activities. Some species also tend to be fairly busy later in the afternoon if there's still plenty of sunlight.

* Listen. Woodpeckers are among the noisiest species of birds. Their sound is fairly distinctive: a fast, repeated drumming against a wood surface. This sound can be louder if the tree is dead and hollow but still fairly solid. You'll hear it for a few seconds, and then it will stop, start again, and then stop. This is the bird's standard drumming pattern. Once you recognize the sound, you won't forget it. Being able to identify it is probably the easiest and quickest way to locate a woodpecker.

* Look for the holes. While on safari, you may not hear the woodpecker's drumming sound. If that's the case, use your binoculars to search for nesting holes. Remember that woodpeckers always leave evidence of their presence: roughly cut holes with splintered edges located high up in both live and dead trees. If you can spot a few of these, then you know you're on the right track for locating a woodpecker.

* Don't make too much noise or movement. Woodpeckers, like most other wild animals, aren't exactly thrilled to be in the company of humans. Once you've located a woodpecker (or several), find a good observation spot and quietly stay there. If you're quiet and don't move, the woodpeckers will relax and go about their business, which is exactly what you want on safari.

* Be patient. You may not spot a woodpecker within the first ten minutes of your safari. That's fine. Woodpeckers are experts at sensing danger, which means they'll probably know you're there long before you know they are.

* Keep your camera ready at all times. It's always rewarding to capture a few great pictures of woodpeckers in the wild, so you need to be ready for such opportunities. Keep your camera on and at the ready. You never know when you will spot a woodpecker, and you may only have a short time to take a picture before the bird flies off. Also, keep your flash off. A sudden bright light could easily scare off a wary woodpecker.

* Make notes. While observing the woodpeckers, write down any information that you feel is important. What were they doing? Where were you when you saw them? What time of day was it? After you gather enough information, you'll begin to recognize patterns that will help you with future safaris.

* Download any pictures (or videos, if you were able to record any) you took when you return home. Show them to your friends and family. You could also write a formal journal using both your pictures and your notes. Keep an ongoing record of your woodpecker safaris from year to year.

THREE

A Guide to Woodpeckers

There are many species of woodpecker throughout North America, as well as numerous subspecies. They vary tremendously in appearance, which makes them relatively easy to identify. There are other birds within the woodpecker family, such as the *Picidae*, that are not known as woodpeckers. Members of this family include sapsuckers, piculets, wrynecks, and flickers.

Refer back to the notes you made while on your safari. Use them to point out **characteristics** of the birds that can help you identify certain species. Consider the following questions:

* What was the woodpecker's basic (base) coloration?
* What were the colors of the feathers on its head?
* Was it near a nest and/or a mate? If so, where was the nest? (If the nest was not in a tree hole, chances are it did not belong to a woodpecker.)

❋ Are there markings on the chest, or is the chest basically one color?

❋ Was the bird clinging to the side of a tree or on the ground? (Woodpeckers do come to the ground from time to time, but not often.)

WOODPECKER
Color(s): black body, reddish-orange head, and white markings
Size: medium
Location: the side of a tree
Activity: drumming and then resting

Using the answers to these questions, look at the next page and see if any of the woodpeckers in the photos match the characteristics you saw. Remember that you should use other information such as your location (town, state, or country) and the time of year that your observations were made. Try doing a little research on the Internet, too. The resources provided in this book's "Find Out More" section are great places to start.

Yellow-bellied Sapsucker

Pileated Woodpecker

Downy Woodpecker

Northern Flicker

FOUR

Try This!
Projects You Can Do

You can't keep woodpeckers as pets, and you certainly can't live with them. You can, however, further your interest in woodpeckers in other hands-on ways when you're not busy on one of your safaris. The following are a few easy and fun projects you can do at home.

Mealtime

Woodpeckers need to eat every day and will appreciate any help you can give them with finding food.

What Do I Need?

- ❋ A standard birdfeeder
- ❋ Small fruits, such as cherries, strawberries, bayberries, elderberries, blueberries, grapes, and raspberries
- ❋ Mealworms (can be purchased in nearly any pet shop)
- ❋ Suet, a hard and fatty mammal tissue found in cows and sheep (can be purchased in most pet shops with bird supplies)

Woodpeckers will happily accept food from a feeder that you've provided.

What Do I Do?

* First, stock your birdfeeder with your chosen food. If you can purchase them, mealworms are fairly healthy for woodpeckers. Woodpeckers also are particularly fond of suet, but they will certainly appreciate any of the above foods.

* Keep a careful watch on the feeder to make sure other animals don't steal the food before the woodpeckers get a chance to feed. Your woodpeckers will be particularly grateful if you place food out during the colder months when food items in the wild are much harder to find.

A Place of Their Own

Building a birdhouse for woodpeckers, and then watching them inhabit it, can be a fun experience.

What Do I Need?

* Wood
* A hammer and nails or wood glue
* Tree or pole
* Ladder
* An adult to help, especially with any power tools you may need

What Do I Do?

❊ Once you have gathered your materials, begin assembling your birdhouse. Unlike some birds, woodpeckers prefer a fair amount of cover, so the birdhouse will need to have a base, roof, and four walls. Both the base and roof need not be any larger than 8 inches (20 cm) square. The walls should be no more than 10 inches (25 cm) tall. Two of the walls should be 8 inches (20 cm) wide and placed at opposite sides of the house. The other two should be cut to fit the space on the base between the two

Building a birdhouse for your local woodpeckers can be a lot of fun—but don't try it without the help of an adult.

Woodpecker Emergency

During one of your safaris, you may encounter a woodpecker that is sick or has been wounded. A hurt woodpecker would either be moving unusually slow or lying on the ground and hardly moving at all. You may be tempted to get closer to the bird to try and help. Don't! You could frighten it so badly that it would become even more sick. The bird may also be carrying a disease that can be very harmful. Ask the adult with you to call your town's local animal control organization (most towns have them), the zoo, or the police department. If you see a woodpecker that is suffering, be smart and have someone else take care of the situation. Don't try to handle it on your own.

walls. When you attach the roof, put it slightly at an angle. Cut a fairly large hole for the woodpecker to enter and exit in one of the walls. Make sure this hole is situated closer to the top than to the base.

❋ When the house is finished, you should place it at the top of a pole (again, with an adult's help) and put it in a quiet section of your yard, preferably near trees. It should be at least 10 feet (3 meters) off the ground, although hanging it even higher from a tree will work well.

Communication

A woodpecker does not peck at trees just to make holes. It also pecks to communicate with other woodpeckers. Communication between animals in the wild is one of their most fascinating and complex behaviors. But you don't need to be a woodpecker to take advantage of this on your safari!

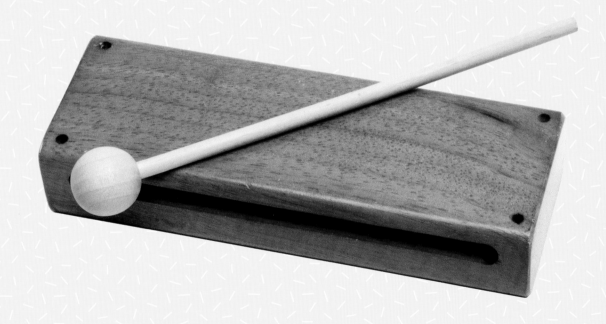

You can catch the attention of a woodpecker by imitating its noises.

What Do I Need?

❋ Woodblock (a block that is hollow is particularly good because it will make a louder sound)

❋ Stick

What Do I Do?

❋ While on safari in the woods, stop quietly and then tap rapidly and hard on the block a few times (the faster the better). You just might fool a woodpecker into doing the same on a tree in order to respond to you. The woodpecker should then be easy to find.

❋ Use the Internet to locate sound files of whatever species of woodpecker occur in your area. The closer you can get to copying the woodpecker's sound, the more success you're likely to have in finding it.

Glossary

arboreal — living, or often found, in trees

characteristic — a specific trait or quality that an animal has, such as tan fur or brown eyes

clutch — a nest of eggs

diurnal — active during the day

habitat — the exact type of place in which an animal lives, such as a burrow, cave, or shoreline

invertebrate — an animal that does not have a backbone

omnivorous — an animal that eats both plant and animal matter

ornithology — the study of birds

predator — an animal that hunts other animals for food

prey — any animal that is hunted by another as food

range — the general area in which an animal lives

species — one type of animal or plant within a larger category

territorial — a word that describes an animal that is protective of the area in which it lives

wingspan — the length of a bird's wings from tip to tip when fully extended

zygodactyl — a bird's foot which has two toes pointing forward and two backward

Find Out More

Books

Cate, Annette LeBlanc. *Look Up! Bird-Watching in Your Own Backyard*. Somerville, MA: Candlewick Press, 2013.

Porter, Adele. *Wild About Northeastern Birds: A Youth's Guide*. Cambridge, MN: Adventure Publications, 2010.

Truit, Trudi Strain. *Birds*. New York: Cavendish Square, 2011.

Websites

The Pileated Woodpecker / National Geographic

kids.nationalgeographic.com/kids/animals/creaturefeature/pileatedwoodpecker

This website offers lots of basic information about one of the most common and widespread American woodpeckers. There are also beautiful photos, a range map, and audio files of various woodpecker sounds.

American Woodpecker Facts for Kids / NatureMapping Program

naturemappingfoundation.org/natmap/facts/pileated_woodpecker_712.html

This website offers excellent details about the Pileated woodpecker species, and includes great photos.

North American Woodpeckers

www.birds-of-north-america.net/woodpeckers.html

Identify North American species of the *Picidae* family while enjoying the many beautiful color photos presented on this website.

Index

Page numbers in **boldface** are illustrations.

About the Author

WIL MARA is the award-winning author of more than 150 books. He began his writing career with several titles about herpetology—the study of reptiles and amphibians. Since then he has branched out into other subject areas and continues to write educational books for children. To find out more about Mara's work, you can visit his website at www.wilmara.com.

ANACONDAS

by Golriz Golkar

Cody Koala

An Imprint of Pop!

popbooksonline.com

abdopublishing.com

Published by Pop!, a division of ABDO, PO Box 398166, Minneapolis, Minnesota 55439. Copyright © 2019 by POP, LLC. International copyrights reserved in all countries. No part of this book may be reproduced in any form without written permission from the publisher. Pop!™ is a trademark and logo of POP, LLC.

Printed in the United States of America, North Mankato, Minnesota

042018
092018

 THIS BOOK CONTAINS RECYCLED MATERIALS

Cover Photo: ER Degginger/Science Source
Interior Photos: Shutterstock Images, 5 (top), 5 (bottom left), 6, 13; Steve Cooper/Science Source, 5 (bottom right); iStockphoto, 9; Yoshiharu Sekino/Science Source, 10–11; M. Watson/Science Source, 15; Sandro Campardo/Keystone/AP Images, 16; Gerard Lacz/Science Source, 19; Chris Mattison/FLPA/Science Source, 20

Editor: Meg Gaertner
Series Designer: Laura Mitchell

Library of Congress Control Number: 2017963421

Publisher's Cataloging-in-Publication Data

Names: Golkar, Golriz, author.
Title: Anacondas / by Golriz Golkar.
Description: Minneapolis, Minnesota : Pop!, 2019. | Series: Rain forest animals | Includes online resources and index.
Identifiers: ISBN 9781532160240 (lib.bdg.) | ISBN 9781532161360 (ebook) |
Subjects: LCSH: Anaconda--Juvenile literature. | Constrictors (Snakes)--Juvenile literature. | Rain forest animals--Juvenile literature. | Rain forest animals--Behavior--Juvenile literature.
Classification: DDC 591.734--dc23

Hello! My name is

Cody Koala

Pop open this book and you'll find QR codes like this one, loaded with information, so you can learn even more!

Scan this code* and others like it while you read, or visit the website below to make this book pop.

popbooksonline.com/anacondas

*Scanning QR codes requires a web-enabled smart device with a QR code reader app and a camera.

Table of Contents

Chapter 1

Big Snake

Anacondas are huge yellow, green, or brown snakes. They have spots and a black stripe on their heads. They have thick necks and narrow heads.

Watch a video here!

5

Anacondas spend time in water. Their eyes and nose are on top of their heads. They can breathe and look for **prey** while they are swimming.

Some anacondas weigh more than a piano!

Chapter 2

Slithering Along

Anacondas lie in the sun to get warm. Sometimes they hang from trees. They also **slither** into water, where they can move more easily than on land.

Learn more here!

Anacondas are **constrictors**. They hide in the dark water. They wait for an animal to come near.

Then they wrap themselves
quickly around their prey.

They squeeze their prey instead of biting it. They eat fish, birds, and even deer. They open their jaws wide and swallow their prey whole!

After a meal, anacondas can go for months without eating.

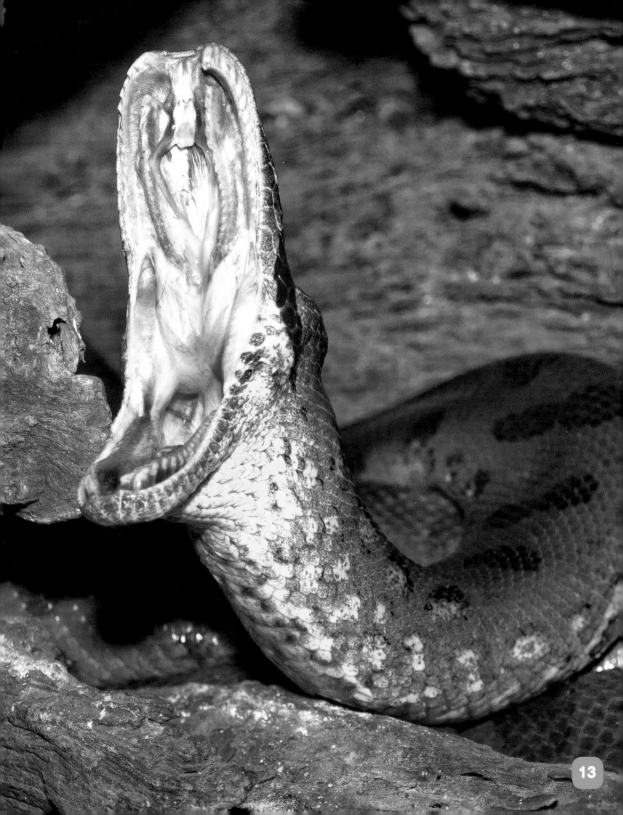

Chapter 3

The Life of an Anaconda

Male anacondas struggle against each other for a **female**'s attention. Often the strongest male wins. Other times the female chooses the winner.

Complete an activity here!

Unlike most snakes,

anacondas do not lay eggs.

Instead, babies grow inside

the mother for six to seven months. The mother has 20 to 40 babies. Baby anacondas live by themselves. They live for about ten years in nature.

Chapter 4

A Snake's Home

Anacondas live in rain forests and swamps in South America. They live in wet, warm, and leafy areas.

Learn more here!

There are no animals that hunt anacondas. People sometimes get scared and kill them needlessly. People should leave anacondas alone to be safe.

Making Connections

Text-to-Self

Have you ever seen a snake at a zoo or in the wild? What did you think of it?

Text-to-Text

Have you read about other animals that swim? Why do different animals spend time in water?

Text-to-World

Sometimes people hurt animals when they are afraid. How can people become less afraid of certain animals? Where can they learn more about these animals?

Glossary

constrictor – a snake that kills its prey by wrapping tightly around it.

female – a person or animal of the sex that can have babies or lay eggs.

male – a person or animal of the sex that cannot have babies or lay eggs.

prey – an animal that is hunted, caught, or eaten by another animal.

slither – to move along the ground on one's stomach by twisting from side to side.

Index

Online Resources

popbooksonline.com

Thanks for reading this Cody Koala book!

Scan this code* and others like it in this book, or visit the website below to make this book pop!

popbooksonline.com/anacondas

*Scanning QR codes requires a web-enabled smart device with a QR code reader app and a camera.